Lindsay A. Lee

HELD
BY
DARKNESS,

◆

EMBRACED
BY
LIGHT

A Collection
of Writings

To my Zoe & Miles, you are the purest forms of love & light.
To my Mom, for always holding space for my dreams.
To Bryce and Chase, you were my first lessons in joy. To my siblings
& Sixters, thank you for your quiet love.

And to all who have inspired my growth- through lessons of joy,
sadness, loss, and vulnerability - thank you.

TABLE OF CONTENTS

DARKNESS

AWAKENING

Light

Balance

DARKNESS

HER AWAKENING

She sat there, waiting. Waiting for what, she couldn't say, but her stillness was absolute- deathly quiet, as though movement might shatter the fragile moment. A silent resolve settled over her like a heavy cloak. For years, she had been waiting- waiting for something to change, for the world to shift, for herself to feel whole.

But did she even know who she was?

"Who am I?" She wondered.

The question stirred within her, soft at first, then louder, until it demanded acknowledgement.

"Who am I?" she asked again, this time aloud, the words echoing in the stillness.

The sound of her own voice startled her, cutting through the quiet like a sudden crack of thunder.

Did she feel that?

Something shifted, deep and low, like the first rumblings of an earthquake. Perhaps it was the sheer weight of the question hanging in the air, or the unexpected sharpness of her voice in the stillness. Whatever it was, it stirred something she hadn't felt in years - something raw, something alive.

It simmered at first, faint and unfamiliar, but it began to build. Slowly at first, like steam rising in a kettle, then faster, hotter, pressing against the walls of her chest until it demanded release.

She stood, her legs trembling, her breath shallow, as if her body could no longer contain it.

"Who the fuck am I?"

The words ripped from her throat, raw and jagged, and as they left her lips, a sound followed-low, primal, and guttural. It was not just a scream but a release, the unfiltered agony of years spent silent.

It was the sound of pain.
Of regret.
Of a woman awakening.

And once it started, she couldn't stop.

The tears came first, hot and relentless, spilling down her cheeks as if they had been waiting for permission. And then the words-messy, tangled, broken, each that had been held back burst forth like a dam finally giving way.

"I've wasted...I've wasted...I've wasted so much time!"

Her voice cracked under the weight of the truth, and she doubled over, clutching her chest, her sobs consuming the

empty room. The heaviness of every lost moment, every hes-
itation, every buried part of herself pressed down, forcing
her to confront it all.

She felt everything—every ounce of sorrow she had carried
in silence, every fragment of rage she had swallowed, every
ache of time slipping away. And yet, beneath the storm of
emotion, something new began to emerge. It was faint at
first, almost imperceptible.

A spark.

A flicker of something stronger, something unfamiliar.
Her breathing began to slow, the tears ebbing like a receding
tide. And in the stillness that followed, a strange clarity set-
tled over her.

A quiet, persistent whisper rose from deep within: This is
not the end.

The pain, however, not ready to let her go, wrapped her in
its grip, pulling her to her knees and curling her into a tight
ball of anguish. Each breath came jagged, every sob wreck-
ing her body until she lay motionless on the floor.

Seconds passed.

Minutes.

Maybe hours.

Time became irrelevant; space disappeared. There was only the void, vast and consuming.

Her body lay limp, soft, and still.

Like a distant echo, a deeper instinct returned. She began to take slow, shuddering breaths. Each inhale pulled her a little closer to herself. Slowly, she flexed her fingers, waiting for her vision to clear.

As her vision cleared, a thought struck her: I don't want to lose this pain.

She didn't want to forget. She wanted to hold onto it, to burn the sharpness of it into her memory, so she would never allow herself to return to this place.

Because forgetting the pain meant forgetting the choices, the moments, the silence that had led her here. And she couldn't afford that.

In this moment, she needed to feel it all—the ache, the loss, the rawness of being stripped bare. She needed to see herself as she truly was:

Lost.
Silent.
Hurting.
Alone.
But awakening.

WHERE I THRIVE

I am the saddest thing I have ever seen.
My pain knows no bounds.
Your trials and tribulations
pale in comparison to mine,
for I carry a lifetime of chaos
too vast to explain.

I cannot hear your hurt
without drowning it in my own.
I cannot hold space
without taking up yours.

My tears run free,
Falling with every inhale,
a wellspring of sorrow
on constant command.

I am the victim.
I have been victimized.
My story plays on repeat—
a loop I cannot escape.
This is my space, where I live,
where I thrive.

I know nothing beyond the title I claim,
but I claim it with pride.
I earned it with every ounce of pain,
with every wound I carry.
I cannot escape my past,
nor do I reach for the future.

I'll remain in the shadow of what was,
a place where sorrow feels like home.
For here, in the quiet darkness,
I am safe from the unknown.

THE PRISON SHE BUILT

Cowardice.

This is how she sees herself.

As a coward.

She wants to escape—from her life, from the fake love—but she is afraid.

She is afraid to destroy the fragile structure that is her life.

She is a coward.

Someone who fears being alone.

Someone who prefers the illusion of comfort over the uncertainty of the unknown.

So she exists in this space.

Not living, merely existing.

Without joy, her life limited to mere existence, trapped in her mind.

Imagining how life could be—somewhere else, with someone else.

Yet, she stays.

In secret, in silence, waiting for her world to implode, even hoping.

So that she might escape her self-imposed prison and learn to live on her own.

Lindsay A. Lee

THE QUIET BETRAYAL OF TIME

Time flows, soft as breath,
slipping from "is" to "was,"
no effort, no fight—
just the quiet betrayal of moments.

I am torn,
inner whispers colliding with outer storms,
a symphony of chaos trying to speak truths
I cannot name.

Feelings rush,
wave after wave,
unstoppable, unrelenting,
filling every corner of my being
with words that sound like mine
but taste like ours.

Who is ours?
Whose voice lingers in the echoes of my own?
What thread ties me to the unseen,
the unknown within?

I wait—
for the combustion, the collapse,
the unveiling of the fraud I fear I am.
Unlucky, unloved, undeserving.

Yet, is it not possible,
just possible,
to become more than this?
To grow beyond the confines of doubt,
to be vast,
Boundless,
Awake?

What will this energy make of me?
Will it crush me,
or transform me?
Will I fracture into nothingness,
or bloom into everything I could be?

Time passes easily,
but I remain here,
searching for the answer
hidden in the space between
who I was
and who I might become.

Lindsay A. Lee

DENIAL

Do you feel that?
No...
Breathe in. Try again.
Do you feel it?

It's every feeling you've buried,
every moment you deny.
Fragments of yourself you refuse to remember.
Deny.
Deny.
Deny.

But you can't hide it forever.
You can't pretend it doesn't exist.
You can only glide through life for so long
before the emotion breaks loose.

It shows itself in your reactions,
in the sharpness of your tongue,
in the way each drink pulls the truth closer to the surface.
And tomorrow, you'll apologize again.

Aren't you tired of apologizing?
Aren't you exhausted from the lies?
There's no calm in the chaos,
only walls you've built to keep the pain at bay.
There's no peace in your restless dreams,
just constant reminders of what you've tried to forget.

When will you be ready to let go?
When will you break free from your self-imposed chains?
It's time for your awakening.
Say it out loud.
Face your pain.

It's time.

Lindsay A. Lee

SADNESS WAITS FOR ME

She sits in sadness,
letting it sweep through her like an ocean breeze-
cool, constant, unrelenting.
It caresses her body,
prickling her skin with its quiet presence.

Sadness is her confidant.
It whispers softly in her ear,
holds her close,
waiting patiently for her invitation to stay.

It lingers by her bedside,
walks silently beside her,
always ready to return.
Sadness nudges her gently,
influencing her choices,
urging her to retreat,
pleading with her to stay in bed.
Like a jealous lover,
it craves all her attention,
savoring the solitude it shares with her.

Needing to be seen,
desperate to be felt,
sadness pushes everything else away.
It casts a shadow,
dimming the light of hope,
of joy,
of love.

She lays still in shadows cast,
enveloped by its embrace,
as it softly whispers,
subtly shaping her fate-
gently nudging,
quietly pushing,
hope, joy, and love away.

CRASH

She writes and she breathes. She breathes and she writes. She writes until the words come flowing out of her like giant waves crashing from the ocean. She is the current, the waves are her, and she is crashing in. She is filled with raw emotion, emotion from a history that she can't move past, and from a future that she is unsure will be. She wants to see herself clearly, as crystal clear as the water. She thinks like the ocean. She thinks that she should have no ending, no beginning, that she should never touch the same place twice. She wants to be as rebellious as the current crashing into thoughts and ideas with no fear, no worries, no second guessing. With simple resilience, with courage and bravery. Stepping into herself with no fear of what others may think.

No one questions the ocean.

No one questions where it goes or how it should be. No one believes that the ocean should be soft and quiet. We simply know that the ocean will be as it is. The ocean embraces its wild and is unbridled with no worry of past, present, or future.

Darling, you were meant to be like the ocean. Untamed, unquestioned, unrestricted. You were meant to flow without touching the same thing twice. You were meant to feel and to change with the season. To become stronger when necessary, to rise higher when needed. You are meant to be unbridled. To crash into the earth and to retreat softer when it is your time to leave.

Crash, darling.

Let yourself be seen, heard, and honored like the ocean. Clean others of their worries, renew, like the ocean. This is meant for you. This is meant for you. You are meant for this.

TIRED

She was tired of the lists. Tired of the organizing, the planning, the endless structure and reason. Every detail, every meticulously crafted plan left her feeling hollow, disconnected from herself.

She couldn't tell where her ego ended and her intuition began. The lines were blurred, tangled in a web of overconsuming judgments. Every thought looped back to what was socially acceptable, to what she should do according to the world's standards.

She was afraid—afraid to let go of the worries, the constant need to do the "right thing," to be the "right woman." But deep down, she knew. She had no idea what it felt like to truly live.

Everything within her screamed for release. Her insides begged her to stop, to learn, to listen—not to the noise of the world, but to her intuition, to the whispers of her soul.

Her spirit called out, pleading with her to reach beyond herself, to discover what it meant to exist outside of the rigid boundaries of her mind. To find solace in connection, to feel so deeply intertwined with the energy around her that she could sense its pulse—hers and others, vibrating as one.

She was so fucking tired of the lists.

Ego

Weakness.
She longs to be acknowledged, to be seen.
She begs, sometimes pleads,
convincing herself she can shape her being
into the person you seek.

Pretending to stand with dignity,
she commands your focus-
unmoved by your convictions.
Her thoughts are loud,
but her voice is louder,
consumed by an intensity
that distorts what is deemed virtuous.

Is it dignity she stands with,
or simply her own need?
The need to feel important,
the desire to be wanted,
to be seen.

UNCLAIMED

Of all the mistakes she made, the greatest was returning to a love that promised to set her free. Too naive to see she was already free, she hadn't yet uncovered the power within her own heart and soul. She didn't yet know that no one could give her what was already hers—the power to define her happiness, the freedom to embrace her individuality, and the courage to live boldly without restraint.

No one held that ability, for her joy was infinite, her spirit unbound.

It was a lesson learned through tribulations and heartache. But with every step she took away from that suffocating love, she uncovered a deeper strength, a boundless joy, and the serenity found in her own peace.

 BLISS

If only the thoughts would fade, and bliss would remain,
She could summon childhood moments, simple and sweet,
Tender memories to quiet the weight of hate.
If only the thoughts would fade, and bliss would remain.

DARK ROAST

Brown guitar.
Earth and ground beneath your feet.
Cowboy hats and lingering sadness.
I release you.

In forgiveness—without malice, without hate—
In peace.

I will remember you as I once did:
Like the Earth,
Sandy and musky,
Grit and ground.
A deep, rich coffee.
The burn and pull of a final cigarette.

And now, I let you go.
You, and the memory of you.

Lindsay A. Lee

LET ME GO

Help me find my release; it's the breath I've held for far too
   long.
Oxygen remains trapped beneath my skin,
fighting to break free and merge with the surrounding
   atmosphere.
I beg you to set me free.
Release me from the mental chaos of depravity.
Liberate me from the shackles of self-hatred and relentless
   self-ridicule.
Free me from the ceaseless inner monologue that insists I
   may never measure up.
Release me from the victimhood of my past and the solitude
   that looms in my future.
I beseech you, release me.
Release me from the relentless thoughts that confine me to
   a dark corner,
offering no hope of escape.
Release me from the caverns of my thoughts and the depths
   of my pain.
Let me break free,
let me move forward.
Please, let me breathe.

AWAKENING

In Stillness, I am Found

Here I am,
Still,
breathing deeply,
exhaling the chaos I once feared,
the pain I dared not name.
I was afraid to feel,
afraid to speak of the weight inside,
unaware that I had vanished,
a shell,
a whisper,
a faint breeze where once I had been a storm.

I grew afraid—
afraid to ask the questions
that might bring the answers I needed,
afraid to know,
afraid to see myself clearly.
When did I learn to hide,
to turn away from my power,
my freedom,
my love?
When did I trade the truth of myself
for shadows that felt safer than the solitude?

But I missed you.
I missed the way it felt to be with you,
to exist within you,
to hear your voice,
to see your light,
to know you as you were,
to accept you as you are.

And now I see—
your love,
your presence,
your truth
were never lost.
I had only forgotten
how to look.

THE QUIET

She didn't realize it, but she was searching for quiet. Her mind was a relentless storm of thoughts—always judging, endlessly assessing, a never-ending stream of chatter. How could she hear her true self beneath all the noise? How could she tend to the cries of her inner child when she was suffocated by "what-ifs"? How would she ever uncover her deepest wants, her real fears, the things she truly loved, or the false hates she had adopted along the way? How could she move past the noise?

She was never still enough to listen. Always moving, planning, and thinking, but never silent. She avoided silence, afraid of what she might face if she stopped. Afraid of what might surface if she dared to sit still. She feared the emotions that might bubble up and force her to feel.

The constant stream of thoughts became her refuge. They shielded her from her past and blurred her present. The chatter was safe. Silence was not.

UNSPOKEN

What can she say that hasn't been said?
She searches for words, grasping at moments,
Hoping for truth in a language that feels hollow.
Are there enough metaphors to capture what she feels?
The right soliloquies,
Or even an idiom that effortlessly holds
The weight of the thoughts circling her mind?

WHEN WE STOPPED LISTENING

The grass whispers stories of those who came before us,
rooting us deeper into the Earth.

But we stopped listening.
Too consumed by the noise to hear the calls of our ancestors.
Too worried about the opinions of others
to sit with the truth of ourselves.

We missed the call—
missed the needs of generations before us,
missed the cries of the land below
and the life around us.

We went about our days swiping and pacifying,
as Mother burned to the ground.
Offering commentary on fleeting conversations,
set to expire within 24 hours,
while life itself—sacred and eternal—
was extinguished beneath us.

So consumed, we stopped hearing.
We stopped feeling.

•

Lindsay A. Lee

When did we lose our connection?
To each other.
To the breathing, living soul of the Earth,
of which we are a part.
To our ancestry,
our history,
our story.

The grass whispers still,
as the roots of the trees grow deeper into the Earth,
begging us to remember
our depth.

THE WEIGHT OF WHAT-IFS

If I am honest, I am afraid.
Not of him, but of me—
Of how I hold myself captive
By holding on to him.

It is casual,
Basic, easy most days,
But he is not my forever.
Comfortable, familiar—
And yet, I am afraid
To leap into something different.

The first jump was chaos,
But it was a happy chaos.
I was free,
Alive,
Living in joy.

Now, I don't know.
Some days I think,
"I could do this.
I could exist here,
In contentment."
Not happiness, but contentment.

Is that enough?

Every sign tells me to let go,
To leave this comfort,
To bury old habits with the past.
Every card says the same,
Yet here I sit,
In the arms of familiarity.

It's not comfort,
But it's easier than the pain
Of letting go.
Easier than
Seeing someone move on,
Breaking a family,
Losing the ties that bind me.

I don't want to be later in life,
Living freely for the first time.
But what if this is it?
What if this is all I get—
No more, no less,
Just this?

What if love is not what I imagined?
Not the movies,
Not the books,
Not the filtered gloss
Of someone else's highlight reel?

This could be it—
The closest I'll ever come.
And sometimes,
That thought
Leaves me so very sad.

THIS VERSION OF ME

I want to dissolve into thought,
to let go of the weight of now
and dream a world
where love spills over,
peace hums softly,
and joy stretches wide like the sky.

I see her there,
this version of me—
Alive,
Open,
creating with abandon,
held by the rhythm of waves
and the secret pulse of forests.
Cabins hidden in the trees,
whispers of waterfalls,
doors that lead to quiet magic.
Every part of me rests there,
building, breathing, being.

But here,
this version—
this heavy, aching self—
I whisper to the unseen.
"This is hard," I say.
"I am tired."

I wonder if I've been here before,
if another me ever felt lighter, freer.
I wonder if this path
was meant to shape me
or break me.
I wonder if I chose it,
or if it chose me.
Some days, the gratitude comes easy—
for my children,
for the flashes of beauty,
for the moments that prove
I can still feel.
But today,
I am stuck.
Rooted in everything I have to do,
the endless cycle of becoming.

I want to stop.
To set it all down,
to let the world turn without me
for just a moment.

Sometimes I pray for direction.
Sometimes I just say thanks.
Most times,
I wonder if anyone is listening at all.

Maybe I've missed the answers,
the small mercies,
the gifts hiding in plain sight.
Maybe this is part of it—
the not knowing,
the stretching,
the waiting.

But I still dream of that other place,
that version of me,
building joy like a fire,
burning bright against the dark.
And maybe,
just maybe,
I can pull her closer—
bring her here.
Make her real.

Lindsay A. Lee

BENEATH THE SUN, AMONG THE ROOTS

Did I hear you?
Not just the sound of words,
but the truth of them,
spoken aloud with an intensity
that rises from the Root,
flows through the Sacral,
and radiates from the Heart.

Unafraid to exist as you are,
boldness unbound,
you bask in the sunlight—
whole enough to be part of the light,
offering a peace that has always eluded me.

Your intensity feels like bravery,
your kindness resonates with the spirit,
grounded and connected to the Earth.

Watching you,
feet in the grass,
soul open,
fully alive—
I am drawn to you.

Held by Darkness, Embraced by Light

I long to know you,
to understand you,
to coexist within your space.
I yearn to share your energy,
to breathe you in.

You are the essence of peace,
of roots,
of home.

Lindsay A. Boulden

SELFISH

I am holding myself back by holding onto him.
And yet, I sit here in easy stillness -
not comfort, perhaps,
but familiarity.

Familiarity feels easier than discomfort,
easier than facing the ache
of watching someone else
move on.

LIGHTS ON

"Leave the lights on,"
his request lingered in her ears,
reverberating through her soul,
stirring fears and vulnerabilities
she could scarcely put into words.

It wasn't just a simple plea-
It was a challenge,
A confrontation with the shadows
she'd long kept hidden.

How could she face this dare,
This quiet demand?

PLEASE

Asking for love beyond measure,
only to receive fragments I cannot keep.
Oh, silly universe,
don't you see?
I want so much more.

BETWEEN BREATH AND BELIEF

I feel so much.
Most of the time, it's emotion bubbling
beneath my skin,
rising from somewhere deep—
beneath my lungs,
below my heart.

It comes first in soft waves,
then tightens, constricting my breath.
I will it down.
I will it.
Yet still, it sits at the back of my throat,
salt pressing against my eyelids,
threatening to spill
onto my cheeks.

I will that away too.
I breathe deeply,
reminding myself of the future,
of the goodness waiting for me,
of the loneliness
that is fleeting,
not forever.

●

Lindsay A. Lee

God has promised me:
Faith.
Hope.
Love.
The greatest of all.

I am grasping onto each—
clinging to faith
with every bit of strength I have,
grasping hope
until my fingers ache,
holding love
until it becomes the marrow of my bones.
This is belief
beyond reason,
intuition that defies logic,
a trust in the unseen.

I breathe,
I wait,
and I believe.

LIGHT

SHE IS JOY

She absolutely radiates. Joy pours from her in waves, crashing through her skin and spilling from her pores like sunlight breaking through clouds. It's undeniable, translucent like tiny bubbles rising to the surface, dancing with the grace of fairies beneath the moonlight.

And her smile-oh, her smile- tells a story of its own. It's a symphony of light, illuminating her face, aligning her body, vibrating with divinity itself. She is God personified, her joy a gift drawn from the deepest well of Spirit.

They ask her, skeptically, almost incredulously: "What did you do? Why are you so happy? Your life is... ordinary. You are just a regular person. Not rich, not famous, not important. Why do you deserve this kind of joy?"

She smiles softly, her voice calm, yet unwavering, and she replies:

"My joy is inherent. It is not tied to wealth, fame, or the measures you value. My joy comes from the love I feel-love that flows from Spirit, through me, and back into the world. The love I feel for you, even through judgment, is everlasting. My love for you transcends the limitations of your perception. It is bigger than who you think I am or who you think I should be. I love because I was created to love.

I was given the gift of life, and with this life, I choose joy.

I choose joy daily- with every breath, every morning I wake, every move I make. I am joyful because I am. What a gift God has given me, to live this life as a spiritual being in human form.

You see my life as ordinary, but I see it as extraordinary. I see magnificence in the smallest moments- in the tireless work of an ant, the laughter of a child, the wisdom of an elder. I see joy in everything, and how lucky am I to experience it?

What about you? What are you lucky for? Where do you see magnificence?

You don't see it, because somewhere along the way, you stopped looking. You stopped believing that the smallest things could bring you joy. You stopped paying attention- to the feel of the wind against your skin, the smell of the rain as it kisses the earth, the rhythmic song of the ocean's waves.

You walk past these moments as if they don't matter, as if they're invisible, searching endlessly for something bigger. But these moments are the bigger. They are greater than the most expensive house, the fastest car, or the grandest adventure.

When you realize that joy is not found out there but within you, everything changes. The search ends, and the discovery begins.

Search yourself. Discover what brings you joy. Dance in the rain. Feel the thunder rumble through your chest. Breathe with the wind. Run with your arms open wide to the world.

Find your joy. It has been waiting for you."

DISCOVERING HER

"Lay," he told her, his voice a soft command. "Lay on your back. Breathe out until there is nothing left, until the air escapes you completely. Breathe until your spine melts into the mattress, until your body surrenders to the sheets."

"Lay," he repeated. "Lay and be still. Be as still as the night sky. And when you feel my breath brushing against your ankles, don't move. Stay. Even if your skin prickles, even if goosebumps rise, just lay. Be still. When your body wants to shift, resist. When your legs beg to writhe, stay anchored. Be still."

"As you lay, I will join you here," he murmured, his words carrying both plea and promise. "Let me lay with you. Let my fingers graze the edges of your skin, tracing places you've forgotten exist."

"Just lay," he whispered, the sound barely brushing the air. "Lay while I uncover you, piece by piece. Lay while I learn the map of your body, every dip, every curve, every secret written in the language of your skin. Let me taste you, slowly, deliberately, until you feel known in ways words cannot reach."

Darling, just lay. Let me follow my fingers with the kiss of my lips, each one a quiet vow to discover more of you. Just lay as I trace the quiet mysteries of your body, as I see you, truly see you.

Please," he breathed, his voice low and tender, "let me lay with you."

TAKE UP SPACE

She wanted to completely fill a space—not with her body, but with her being. She longed to expand beyond the edges of herself, to become bigger than she had ever imagined. The size she craved wasn't physical; it was something deeper. She wanted her energy to spill over, radiating outward, touching everyone within reach.

She envisioned herself that way—big, vibrant, alive. A force of nature, radiant and electric, an undeniable presence. But when she caught her reflection, the image didn't match the vision. Instead, she saw someone plain, unassuming, invisible. She felt like a shadow, barely noticed, barely there.

She couldn't pinpoint when it began, this slow fading of herself. Maybe it was in middle school, when she tried so hard not to be noticed that she succeeded too well. She learned to shrink, to hover in corners, to disappear under hoodies. She became the quiet one, the invisible one, more likely to be found watching than participating, more likely to linger on the edges than take her place in the center.

At home, she withdrew into her room, her safe space. There, she could dream of the person she wanted to be. She would sit in quiet conversation with the version of herself that felt impossible to reach—bold, confident, worthy.

She didn't know it yet, but maybe she would. Someday, hopefully, she would see that she had always been enough. That she had the right to take up space, just as she was.

She didn't need to check boxes, to meet some impossible standard, or to prove her worth. She didn't have to be louder, thinner, or more accomplished to exist fully in this world. She could fill any space—not by changing herself, but by embracing herself. Her kind, quiet energy was enough. Her presence was enough.

Maybe she would realize that perfection wasn't necessary. She didn't need to be polished or remarkable or armed with stories of adventure and success to belong.

She simply had to be. To breathe, to exist, to allow herself to take root in the spaces she once thought she didn't deserve. She was already worthy—worthy of being seen, of being felt, of being here.

MORE

She wanted more. She was exhausted—tired of the bullshit, tired of the monotony, tired of searching for answers she could never seem to find. Tired of not knowing who she truly was.

She craved more. More life, more feeling, more fire. She wanted to be known for more—more than a mother, more than a friend, more than a wife. Deep down, she understood that these titles, while meaningful, were not enough. They did not even begin to hold the weight of who she was.

Because at her core, she was power.

She was emotion, raging fire, and fierce winds. She carried the depth of the ocean within her, infinite and unknowable. She was more than words, more than roles, more than expectations.

She was all things.

Every feeling, every song, every poem, every piece of art ever created—she was the essence of them all. A force so vast, so boundless, that no title, no simple word, could ever contain her. She knew it, felt it deep in her bones, in her soul. This is why she could not settle.

This is why she felt she would always be searching. Searching for her purpose, diving endlessly into the pursuit of understanding. Book after book, journal after journal, always seeking answers. Yet, the answers she sought had always been there, hidden in the quiet spaces within her.

It would take time, but one day she would realize—she didn't need to search.

She just needed to be still.

To be still, to listen, and to remember who she already was.

HIGHER

You stand at the threshold of something new—
something you may not have felt fully ready to embrace,
acknowledge, or even envision.
You are on the verge of a transformation,
one that will redefine who you are
and elevate you to a frequency beyond what you thought
    possible.

Your energy vibrates higher now,
your soul radiates with newfound vitality.
The love you give and receive has deepened,
woven into the very essence of who you are—
stronger, brighter, more alive than ever before.

In this moment, you exist as the highest expression of
    yourself,
poised to give and receive in abundant beauty.
Step boldly into the future, leaving the past behind.
This space, this moment, has been carefully crafted for your
    growth.

Embrace the journey into the unknown—
for it is the gateway to your remarkable new existence.

Lindsay A. Lee

UNSHACKLED

She is the sun—
radiant, warm, and alive.
Her glow ignites passions,
her soul unshackled from earthly bonds,
unburdened by fear or doubt.

She dances with the breeze,
fluid and untamed,
like the wind itself.

Oh, to be like the wind—
wild and carefree,
a wandering spirit.
Whispering through canyons,
softly kissing windows,
running through meadows,
and boldly embracing the unknown.

What secrets does she carry?
What mysteries does she hide?

She is unbounded and free,
moving in harmony with nature,
unknowingly composing a symphony all her own.

PHOENIX

Burn it all down. Burn it to the ground—you can have it all. She no longer wanted the façade, the curated lifestyle, the life built on expectations rather than her own desires. The clothes, the style, the image—it was all a lie. None of it fit who she truly was. Take it. The path that was expected. The career that was respected. The safe, predictable life. Even the sex—ordinary, routine—when deep down she craved something wild, something real, something more.

None of it was enough.

Burn it down.

The meal times, the schedules, the daily routines—all of it so regular, so safe. But she... she was exceptional. She was chaos intertwined with creativity, less vanilla and more fire. She was lazy mornings and sleepless nights, poetry and passion, deep conversations and raw freedom.

She was ready to let it all go.

She was ready to burn her life to the ground for a chance to truly live.

Lindsay A. Lee

No Map, No Master

I belong to me.
I release the weight of the status quo,
    of expectations, of tradition.
My soul calls for more—my spirit, restless for centuries, has
    tried again and again to live in joy, in freedom, in love.
To rise, higher and higher, until I reach
    the fullest expression of myself.

I have been reaching for her—this peaceful version of me.
The one who is free.
Free to love, to exist as she is.
Free to say yes at will, to state no
    without apology or explanation.
Free to embrace her power, her energy, her gifts—
To offer no atonement for the path she chooses to walk.

I long for the freedom she has—
To owe no one an explanation,
To chart my course without offering a map.

To redefine normalcy,
To embrace rebellion, mysticism, and the wisdom
    hidden in shadows.
To let intuition be my guide,
To break free from every mental, spiritual,
    and emotional restraint.

This journey is mine alone.
Choice and courage—
These are the sacred gifts I have been given.

Lindsay A. Lee

PEACE WITHIN

She once craved stillness to find her peace,
The softness of grass to feel connected,
Positive words to feel validated,
And the touch of others to feel love.

Now, she finds it all within herself.
Her love is inherent, her peace rooted deep inside.
She knows she is connected to everything around her,
And her need to be seen has faded,
Drifting away with the remnants of her ego.

She has discovered herself—
Full, whole,
Inherently worthy.

I See You

She sometimes felt unseen. Often wondering if anyone saw beneath the surface. She didn't understand how she could feel so alone in a crowded room. So different. At times she wanted to scream from the top of her lungs;

"Do you get me?"

"Do you see me?"

"Do you accept me as I am?"

She saw herself as bruised and scarred, wild and tame. She was willing to dance wildly beneath the stars in an effort to connect to something bigger, something vast. She lit incense and curated moon water under the full moon. She dealt in crystals and vibrations to feel some sort of connection. She asked ancestors for guidance and spirit for reason because it brought her peace and understanding.

She didn't weep for herself, she wept for the nothingness in those around her. They were missing their connection to something bigger. They were so busy moving that they didn't feel their oneness with the Earth. Too busy to feel the sun or to experience the power of bare feet on the ground.

But she would continue to love them all. Regardless of judgements or opinions, hatred or fear. She would continue to love them as she loved herself.

A Day Without Time

Just for today, she allowed herself to exist in the cocoon of him. Just for today, she let herself feel what she thought was long gone. She felt seen—the way he looked at her made her feel sexy, alive, valued, and heard. Yes, truly seen.

For so long, she had convinced herself that what she truly longed for wasn't meant for her. Lost in thought, she had resigned to creating the energy in her mind, knowing those thoughts were the closest she would ever come. But now, she had what she had asked for. She had received what she had created. The universe placed him in her path, and just for today, she felt everything she had dreamed of.

She understood that all things have an expiration date. But just for a day, she existed in a pure, untouched bubble of love.

Just for today. Just for a moment.

But it was hers. It was her moment.

BALANCE

HELD BY DARKNESS, EMBRACED BY LIGHT

She thought the darkness was her enemy,
a shadow pulling her deeper into herself,
a weight she could not carry,
a void she could not escape.

But the darkness was not a thief.
It did not take her power or strip her of her worth.
It held her, gently, firmly,
offering a cocoon for her pain,
a space to grieve,
to scream,
to break apart.

It was in that breaking
that she found her light.
Not in running,
not in resistance,
but in surrendering to the shadows,
letting them cradle her as she fell.

And when the light returned—
not as a flash,
but as a soft, steady glow—
she realized the darkness had never abandoned her.
It had only prepared her to see,
to feel,
to hold herself
with the same tenderness it had offered.

She was held by darkness,
but she was never trapped.
She was embraced by light,
but she was never incomplete.

She had always been both.
Light and dark,
grief and joy,
chaos and peace.

She was not saved by the light;
she was saved by the wholeness of it all.

RETURN TO ME

I sent for her, desperately begging for her return.
Unabashedly, I pleaded,
"Please, my love, will you come back to me?"

But she remained in the shadows,
Refusing my call,
silent, unmoving,
Turning away from my desperation.

I begged, I cried.
"I never meant to lose you.
How could I have known?
How could I have seen that with every 'yes'
that should have been a 'no,'
I was giving away pieces of myself?
Fragments, small at first,
Until I unraveled completely,
Until I forgot who I once was."

And now, here I sit-
searching, pleading, begging
for the return of the pieces I lost,
for the chances to feel whole again.

Lindsay A. Lee

WRAPPED IN YOUR ENERGY

Do you feel that?
The way it feels to kiss—
sweet lips on lips, wrapped in your energy.
Sharing secrets we've never spoken,
exploring places we've never been,
and daring to hope in a way we were once too afraid to.

Do you see that?
The way my eyes light up when you're near,
how my breath quickens as you draw closer.
The anticipation.
The excitement.

I want more of it.
Can we hold onto this?
I don't want to lose the way I feel when we kiss.

WHEN 2 R IN RHYTHM

If music is your love language,
Let me learn your inherent rhythm and melodious beat.
I want to be your diary, your favorite piece of music,
A timeless melody etched into your skin.

I'll harmonize with your laughter,
Be a verse in the chaos,
Your chorus in the calm.

I'll be the center of each major or minor,
Perfecting every key.
4/4, 3/4—breathing slowed with each beat.
Play me on demand,
Speak to me in music,
Translating tempos to soft touches,
Building like crescendos.
Creating a Symphony of sound.

Shhhh

As a child, she was often called boisterous.
They said she talked too much,
her voice always a bit too loud.

But she couldn't help it.
Her mind brimmed with questions about the world,
Wonders to explore,
And endless creative ideas.
She needed a way to let the musings spill out,
To release the constant hum of curiosity.

Perhaps if they had encouraged her instead of silencing her,
she wouldn't now carry this fear-
This quiet hesitation-
To trust the power of her own voice.

Lindsay A. Lee

I'VE BEEN LOOKING FOR YOU

She stood in the mirror and asked,
"Where have you been?"

To her she replied,
"I got lost in your shadow."

UNBROKEN

My greatest loss shattered my heart
But it could never shatter me.
No one holds that power over me -
No one can break me.

I am whole.
I am love.
I am neither fragile nor dainty
I am.

Lindsay A. Lee

IN THIS SPACE

In her mind, she created a sanctuary,
a place where she could simply exist.
Here, she was free—
untamed, wild, and unapologetically herself.
In this sacred space, love held her,
not bound by expectations or reason.
She was protected, yet limitless,
unbridled and breathtakingly beautiful.

She was part of everything,
and everything was part of her.
The wind carried her energy,
the trees grounded her power.
She was not just in the world—
she was the world.
In this space, she felt infinite,
whole, and free.

NAKED

He dared her to come to him unclothed, open, and vulnerable. She heard his words, absorbed his challenge, and unknowingly began constructing her walls. She didn't know how to allow herself to be that free. Yet, he dared her again, asking her to dive into the fear and to lay in her discomfort. Challenging her, telling her that he would come to her completely naked and unafraid. He proclaimed that she did not need to meet him halfway, he would come beyond the middle and into her world. He would carry the burden of vulnerability; he simply needed her to trust him.

Slowly she peeled off her layers, unveiling skin and scars. She stepped out of the door and stood before him, fully exposed in body and soul. Feeling the cool breeze against her skin and the excitement running through her veins, she waited. Silent he stood, watching her. His gaze was filled with admiration. Her vulnerability spoke volumes and he understood the weight of her actions. They stood face to face, both stripped down to their true selves unburdened by pretenses. Slowly, he reached out to take her hand. She came to him fully open and into his arms.

THE TRUTH OF HER NATURE

How does a lioness appear?
She moves like a prayer in motion,
graceful and sure,
guided by an inner knowing.
Her strength is quiet yet profound,
rooted in the essence of who she is.

In the stillness of the bushes, she waits—
not with impatience,
but with trust in divine timing.
Her power is not something she wears,
but something she is.
It flows through her effortlessly,
a sacred gift she neither questions
nor seeks to prove.

The lioness carries no need for validation;
her worth is written into her being.
She does not ask permission to fully exist,
nor does she yield to the world's demands.
She simply aligns,
Unwavering,
with the truth of her nature.

Now imagine this for yourself:

What would it mean to embody your power
as gently as a breath,
as steadily as the earth?

To step into your strength,
not with force,
but with a simple certainty—
as if it were always yours,
waiting to be embraced.

Who might you become
if you allowed yourself to be
softly,
fully,
without apology?

ABOUT THE AUTHOR

Lindsay A. Lee is a writer, mentor, and advocate for self-discovery, wellness, and spiritual growth. With a background in education, business, and wellness, Lindsay combines her passion for teaching with her love for storytelling, creating spaces for reflection, empowerment, and transformation. She believes in the power of words to guide others on their journey to embracing purpose, authenticity, and self-love.

As a dedicated mentor and educator, Lindsay draws from her personal experiences and professional insights to inspire women to find balance in life's dualities—navigating the light and dark, joy and sorrow, and growth through vulnerability. Her work reflects a deep understanding of the human experience and the beauty in embracing life's complexities.

When she's not writing or mentoring, Lindsay values time with her children and the people that she loves. She's passionate about fitness and wellness, believing in the vital connection between body and mind in creating a meaningful and balanced life. Lindsay is committed to guiding others toward living fully, freely, and with a sense of inner peace and purpose.